KU-422-043

Animal Top Tens

Australasia's Most Amazing Animals

Anita Ganeri

www.raintreepublishers.co.uk

Visit our website to find out more information about Raintree books.

To order:
☎ Phone 44 (0) 1865 888112
▤ Send a fax to 44 (0) 1865 314091
▢ Visit the Raintree Bookshop at **www.raintreepublishers.co.uk** to browse our catalogue and order online

First published in Great Britain by Raintree, Halley Court, Jordan Hill, Oxford OX2 8EJ, part of Harcourt Education.
Raintree is a registered trademark of Harcourt Education Ltd.

© Harcourt Education Ltd 2008
The moral right of the proprietor has been asserted.

All rights reserved. No part of this publication may be reproduced, stored in a retrieval system, or transmitted in any form or by any means, electronic, mechanical, photocopying, recording, or otherwise, without either the prior written permission of the publishers or a licence permitting restricted copying in the United Kingdom issued by the Copyright Licensing Agency Ltd, 90 Tottenham Court Road, London W1T 4LP (www.cla.co.uk).

Editorial: Nancy Dickmann and Catherine Veitch
Design: Victoria Bevan and Geoff Ward
Illustrations: Geoff Ward
Picture Research: Mica Brancic
Production: Victoria Fitzgerald

Originated by Modern Age
Printed and bound by CTPS (China Translation & Printing Services Ltd)

13-digit ISBN 978 1 4062 0916 7
12 11 10 09 08
10 9 8 7 6 5 4 3 2

British Library Cataloguing in Publication Data
Ganeri, Anita, 1961–
  Australasia's Most Amazing Animals.
(Animal top tens)
  591.9'9
A full catalogue record for this book is available from the British Library.

Acknowledgements
The author and publisher are grateful to the following for permission to reproduce copyright material: ©Ardea pp. **15**, **23** (D. Parer & E. Parer-Cook), **16** (Valerie Taylor), **20** (Don Hadden); ©Ardea/Auscape pp. **4** (Reg Morrison), **8** (Kathie Atkinson); ©Corbis/Reuters p. **7** (David Gray); ©FLPA p. **22** (Chris Mattison); ©FLPA/Minden Pictures pp. **11** (Tui De Roy), **17**, **18** (Norbert Wu), **19**, **27** (Fred Bavendam); ©Getty Images/National Geographic p. **14** (Nicole Duplaix); ©OSF pp. **12** (Tony Tilford), **13** (Densey Clyne), **24** (Robin Smith); ©OSF/Earth Scenes/Animals Animals pp. **6** (Mickey Gibson), **9** (Patti Murray), **21**, **25** (DANI/JESKE N/A), **26** (Werner Layer); ©OSF/Mauritius Die Bildagentur Gmbh p. **10** (Vidler Vidler).

Cover photograph of a tuatara, reproduced with permission of NHPA/Kevin Schafer.

The publishers would like to thank Michael Bright for his assistance with the preparation of this book.

Every effort has been made to contact copyright holders of any material reproduced in this book. Any omissions will be rectified in subsequent printings if notice is given to the publishers.

Disclaimer
All the internet addresses (URLs) given in this book were valid at time of going to press. However, due to the dynamic nature of the Internet, some addresses may have changed, or sites may have changed or ceased to exist since publication. While the author and publishers regret any inconvenience this may cause readers, no responsibility for any such changes can be accepted by either the author or the publishers. It is recommended that adults supervise children on the Internet.

Contents

Australasia...4

Wombat...6

Funnel-web spider.......................................8

Kiwi..10

Birds of paradise..12

Platypus..14

Box jellyfish..16

Leafy sea dragon...18

Tuatara...20

Water-holding frog.....................................22

Thorny devil...24

Animals in danger.......................................26

Animal facts and figures.............................28

Find out more..30

Glossary..31

Index..32

Some words are printed in bold, **like this**. You can find out what they mean on page 31 in the Glossary.

Australasia

Australasia is the world's smallest **continent**. It covers about 7,700,000 sq kilometres (2,972,900 sq miles). Australia makes up most of the continent but Australasia also includes New Zealand, Papua New Guinea, and thousands of tiny islands which are scattered across the Pacific Ocean.

Australasia has many different kinds of landscape. These range from **rainforests** in northern Australia and Papua New Guinea, to snowy mountains in southern New Zealand. Most of the centre of Australia is covered in dry, dusty **desert**. A huge **coral reef**, called the Great Barrier Reef, lies off the north-east coast of Australia.

Australasia is the driest continent on Earth, with much of its land desert.

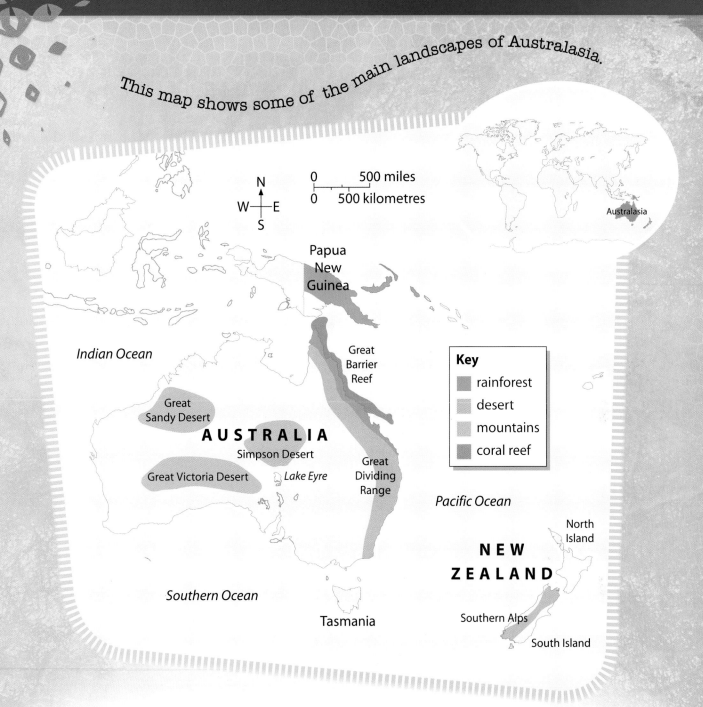

This map shows some of the main landscapes of Australasia.

0 500 miles
0 500 kilometres

N
W E
S

Australasia

Papua
New
Guinea

Indian Ocean

Great
Barrier
Reef

Key
rainforest
desert
mountains
coral reef

Great
Sandy Desert

AUSTRALIA

Simpson Desert

Great Victoria Desert

Lake Eyre

Great
Dividing
Range

Pacific Ocean

North
Island

**NEW
ZEALAND**

Southern Ocean

Tasmania

Southern Alps

South Island

An amazing range of animals has **adapted** to live in these
habitats. Kangaroos, emus, and frilled lizards live in the
desert. The rainforests and woodlands are home to snakes,
butterflies, and koalas. The coral reefs are crowded with
fish, starfish, and shellfish. Many of Australasia's animals
are found nowhere else on Earth.

Wombat

With their round bodies and large heads, wombats look like small bears. Their thick fur is light-brown to grey-black in colour. Wombats live mainly in southern Australia. They come out to feed on grass, roots, and bark at night, when it is cooler.

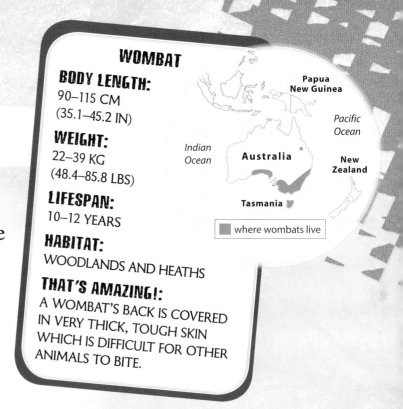

WOMBAT

BODY LENGTH:
90–115 CM
(35.1–45.2 IN)

WEIGHT:
22–39 KG
(48.4–85.8 LBS)

LIFESPAN:
10–12 YEARS

HABITAT:
WOODLANDS AND HEATHS

THAT'S AMAZING!:
A WOMBAT'S BACK IS COVERED IN VERY THICK, TOUGH SKIN WHICH IS DIFFICULT FOR OTHER ANIMALS TO BITE.

Papua New Guinea

Pacific Ocean

Indian Ocean

Australia

New Zealand

Tasmania

where wombats live

Burrows help to keep wombats warm in winter and cool in summer.

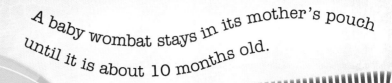
A baby wombat stays in its mother's pouch until it is about 10 months old.

Marsupials

Wombats are **marsupials**. They give birth to tiny young which crawl into their mother's pouch to feed and grow. A wombat's pouch faces backwards so that it does not fill up with soil as the wombat digs.

Champion digger

Wombats like **habitats** where the soil is easy to dig. They dig **burrows** with their strong front paws and claws, and push out the soil with their back legs. Their burrows can be 20 metres (65.6 feet) long and more than 2 metres (6.5 feet) below ground.

Funnel-web spider

Funnel-webs are large spiders. They are found in eastern Australia and Tasmania, in forests along the coast. During the day, they shelter in their **burrows** so that they do not dry up in the heat.

Funnel-web spiders have shiny dark brown or black bodies and long legs.

FUNNEL-WEB SPIDER

BODY LENGTH:
1.5–4.5 CM (.05–1.7 IN)

WEIGHT:
ABOUT 0.8–2 G
(0.02–0.07 OZ)

LIFESPAN:
2–4 YEARS (FEMALE);
9 MONTHS (MALE)

HABITAT:
COASTAL FORESTS

THAT'S AMAZING!:
FUNNEL-WEB SPIDERS RUSH OUT OF THEIR BURROWS WHEN **PREY,** SUCH AS INSECTS AND LIZARDS, DISTURB THE 'TRIP LINES' AROUND THEIR WEBS.

Papua New Guinea

Pacific Ocean

Indian Ocean

Australia

New Zealand

Tasmania

where funnel-web spiders live

Silk 'trip lines' warn the spider of possible prey, mates, and danger.

Spider poison
The funnel-web is one of the world's deadliest spiders. If people are bitten, they feel pain, their mouths go numb and they start to dribble and sweat. If they do not get medical help fast, they can become very ill and die.

Spider burrows

Funnel-web spiders live in burrows under rocks and rotting logs. The burrows have funnel-shaped entrances, and are lined with silky webs. Males leave their burrows in summer to find females to **mate** with. At this time, they sometimes wander into people's homes, gardens, and swimming pools.

Kiwi

The kiwi is a bird that only lives in New Zealand. About the size of a chicken, the kiwi has spiky, red-brown feathers. It lays the largest eggs for the size of its body.

BROWN KIWI

BODY LENGTH:
UP TO 55 CM (21.6 IN)

WEIGHT:
UP TO 3.8 KG (8.4 LBS)

LIFESPAN:
20 YEARS

HABITAT:
COASTAL FORESTS;
GRASSLANDS

THAT'S AMAZING!:
DURING THE NIGHT, A KIWI MAY ROAM ACROSS AN AREA THE SIZE OF 60 FOOTBALL PITCHES IN SEARCH OF FOOD.

where kiwis live

New Zealand

Pacific Ocean

A kiwi egg weighs about a quarter of the kiwi's body weight.

Life on land

The kiwi cannot fly. Over millions of years, kiwis have **adapted** to living on the ground rather than in the air. They can run very fast on their large feet, and although they have small wings they do not use them to fly. Kiwis feed on insects, **larvae,** and worms that live on the forest floor. Most birds use sight to find their food but kiwis use their excellent sense of smell. Their nostrils are at the ends of their long bills for sniffing out food in the dark.

A kiwi searches for food at night.

Birds of paradise

Beautiful birds of paradise live in the **rainforests** of Papua New Guinea and northern Australia. They live high up in the trees, feeding on the many fruits, insects, and spiders that are found in their forest **habitat**.

This bird of paradise has tail feathers 50 cm (20 inches) long.

BIRD OF PARADISE

BODY LENGTH:
17–120 CM (6.7–47.2 IN)

WEIGHT:
50–400 G (1.7–14 OZ)

LIFESPAN:
UP TO 30 YEARS
(IN **CAPTIVITY**)

HABITAT:
RAINFORESTS

THAT'S AMAZING!:
UNLIKE THE MALES, FEMALE BIRDS OF PARADISE ARE A DULL BROWN COLOUR. THIS IS USEFUL BECAUSE IT **CAMOUFLAGES** THEM WHEN THEY ARE SITTING ON THEIR NESTS.

Papua New Guinea

Pacific Ocean

Indian Ocean

Australia

New Zealand

Tasmania

where birds of paradise live

Dazzling display

Male birds of paradise are famous for their colourful feathers. They show these feathers off to compete with other males and win a female. Some birds display their feathers while they dance on the ground. Others hang from tree branches, flapping their wings and fanning out their beautiful tails. The female birds watch the males and choose the ones that they like the most.

Platypus

The platypus is an amazing **mammal** that lives in rivers and streams in eastern Australia. It is one of only five kinds of mammal that lay eggs. The platypus uses its webbed feet like paddles for swimming and its flat tail for steering. It has a leathery, duck-like bill for scooping up worms, shellfish, and insects from the mud on the river bed.

The platypus is clumsy on land but is very well **adapted** for life in the water.

14

Laying eggs

The female platypus builds a nest of grass and leaves in a tunnel in the river bank. Then she lays two to three soft, grape-sized eggs. When the baby platypuses hatch about ten days later, they feed on their mother's milk.

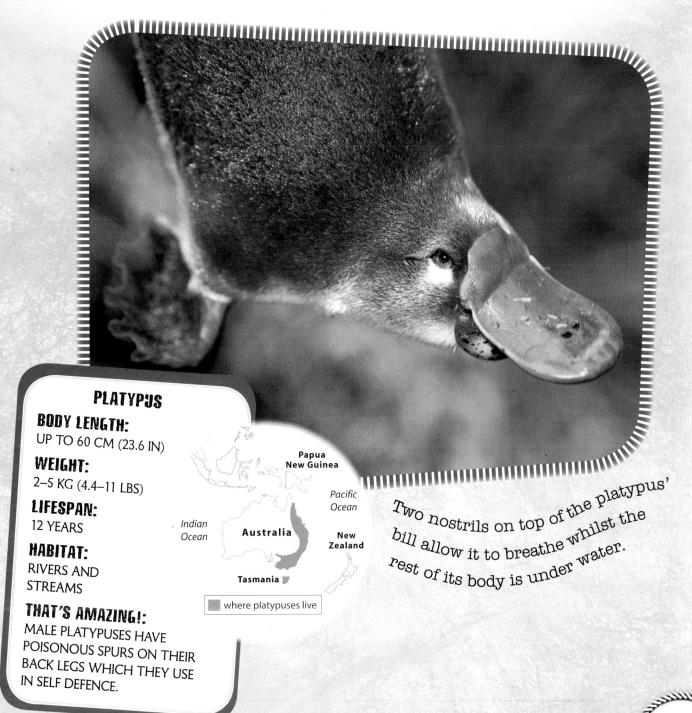

Two nostrils on top of the platypus' bill allow it to breathe whilst the rest of its body is under water.

PLATYPUS

BODY LENGTH:
UP TO 60 CM (23.6 IN)

WEIGHT:
2–5 KG (4.4–11 LBS)

LIFESPAN:
12 YEARS

HABITAT:
RIVERS AND STREAMS

THAT'S AMAZING!:
MALE PLATYPUSES HAVE POISONOUS SPURS ON THEIR BACK LEGS WHICH THEY USE IN SELF DEFENCE.

Papua New Guinea

Pacific Ocean

Indian Ocean

Australia

New Zealand

Tasmania

☐ where platypuses live

Box jellyfish

Box jellyfish live in shallow water off the coast of northern Australia. They are most commonly seen between October and April. They have box-shaped bodies and **tentacles** which measure over 3 metres (9.8 feet). The jellyfish's colour makes it difficult to see in the water.

BOX JELLYFISH

BODY LENGTH:
20 CM (7.8 IN)

WEIGHT:
UP TO 2 KG (4.4 LBS)

LIFESPAN:
LESS THAN 1 YEAR

HABITAT:
COASTS

THAT'S AMAZING!:
FOR SOME REASON, SEA TURTLES ARE NOT HARMED BY BOX JELLYFISH STINGS. THEY OFTEN EAT THE JELLYFISH.

Papua New Guinea

Indian Ocean

Pacific Ocean

Australia

New Zealand

where box jellyfish live

A jellyfish has about 5,000 stinging cells on each of its tentacles.

Deadly sting

The box jellyfish is probably the deadliest animal in the world. Each jellyfish has up to 60 tentacles, growing from the corners of its body. The tentacles are covered in stinging cells which shoot poison into any creature that touches them. The jellyfish normally uses its poison to catch its **prey** of small fish and shellfish. It also uses its poison in self defence. It is so harmful that it could kill a person in less than four minutes.

Special signs on beaches warn swimmers to watch out for jellyfish.

Leafy sea dragon

Leafy sea dragons live among **coral reefs** and seaweed beds off the coasts of southern and western Australia. They feed on shrimp-like creatures which they suck up with their long, straw-like snouts. They use the tiny fins on their necks and backs to swim slowly through the water.

Leafy sea dragons are fish and are closely related to sea horses.

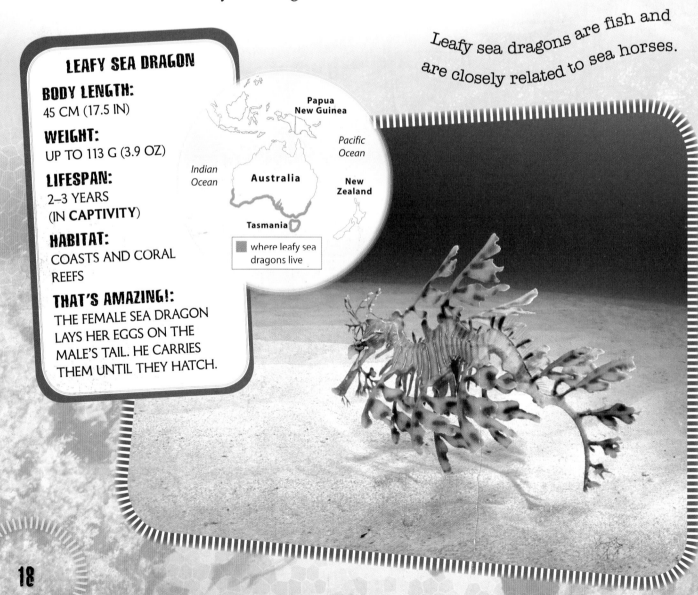

LEAFY SEA DRAGON

BODY LENGTH:
45 CM (17.5 IN)

WEIGHT:
UP TO 113 G (3.9 OZ)

LIFESPAN:
2–3 YEARS
(IN **CAPTIVITY**)

HABITAT:
COASTS AND CORAL
REEFS

THAT'S AMAZING!:
THE FEMALE SEA DRAGON
LAYS HER EGGS ON THE
MALE'S TAIL. HE CARRIES
THEM UNTIL THEY HATCH.

Papua
New Guinea

Pacific
Ocean

Indian
Ocean

Australia

New
Zealand

Tasmania

where leafy sea
dragons live

Cunning camouflage

A leafy sea dragon's body is yellowish-green and is covered in leaf-like flaps of skin. These are not used for movement. Instead, they provide **camouflage** amongst the seaweed that grows in its **habitat**. For extra protection, the sea dragons' bodies are covered in tough plates. They also have long, sharp spines running along their backs.

The sea dragon's camouflage makes it difficult for **predators** to spot.

Tuatara

The tuatara is a very rare **reptile**. It has a long, lizard-like body with a spiny crest running along its back, neck, and head. Its skin ranges from olive-green to grey to dark pink in colour.

TUATARA

BODY LENGTH:
40–60 CM (15.6–23.6 IN)

WEIGHT:
UP TO 1.3 KG (2.8 LBS)

LIFESPAN:
UP TO 100 YEARS

HABITAT:
ISLANDS

THAT'S AMAZING!:
MALE TUATARAS SOMETIMES LOSE THEIR TAILS IN FIGHTS, BUT AMAZINGLY THEY CAN GROW NEW ONES.

where tuataras live

New Zealand

Pacific Ocean

The male tuatara can raise his spines to scare off **predators**.

Tuatara lifestyle

Tuataras live along the coast. They use seabird **burrows** to shelter in during the day. At night, the tuataras come out to look for food. They feed on snails, frogs, lizards, small sea birds, and sea bird eggs and chicks.

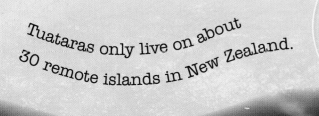

Tuataras only live on about 30 remote islands in New Zealand.

Life cycle

After **mating**, the female tuatara lays 7–10 eggs in an underground nest. The eggs take a long time to hatch (12–15 months). This is because the babies inside stop growing in the winter when they might not survive. They start growing again when the weather gets warmer.

Water-holding frog

The water-holding frog lives in **deserts, grasslands,** and **swamps** in central and southern Australia. It spends most of its life in an underground **burrow** and only comes to the surface after heavy rain.

WATER-HOLDING FROG

BODY LENGTH:
40–70 MM (1.5–2.7 IN)

WEIGHT:
UP TO 20 G (0.7 OZ)

LIFESPAN:
UP TO 20 YEARS

HABITAT:
DESERTS

THAT'S AMAZING!:
THE FROG LAYS ITS EGGS IN PUDDLES LEFT AFTER IT HAS RAINED. THE TADPOLES MUST GROW AND CHANGE INTO FROGS QUICKLY BEFORE THE WATER DRIES UP AGAIN.

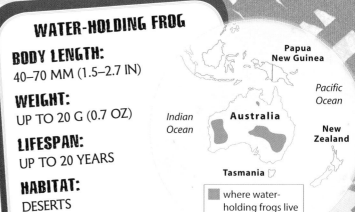

Papua New Guinea

Pacific Ocean

Indian Ocean

Australia

New Zealand

Tasmania

where water-holding frogs live

The water-holding frog is greenish-grey with a fat body and a wide, flat head.

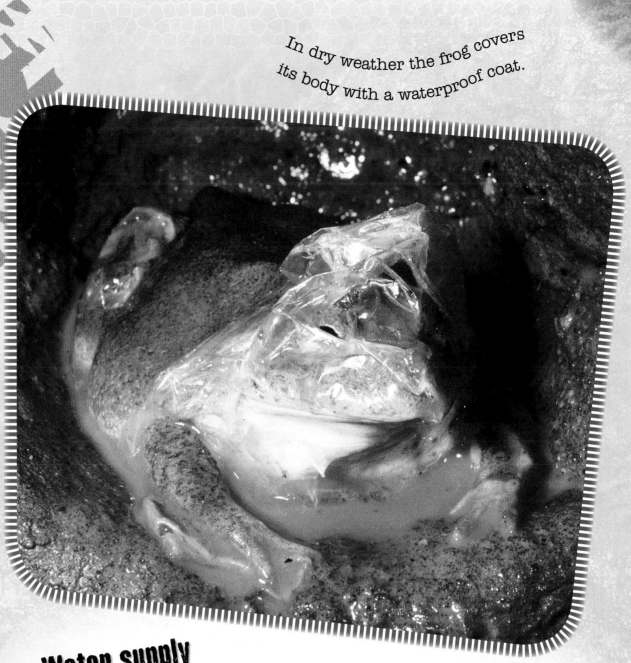

Water supply

The frog has an unusual way of surviving when the weather is hot and dry. It shelters inside an underground burrow and covers its body in a waterproof coat made of dead skin. This coat stops the frog drying out. It stores water in its bladder and in pockets underneath its skin. Using this water store, the frog can survive for months or even years until the rains come.

Thorny devil

The thorny devil looks scary but is actually harmless. The large, sharp spines on its body protect it from attack by **predators**, such as birds. It can also tuck its head between its front legs to make it difficult to swallow. Its brown-yellow colouring helps to hide it among the rocks and sand. It can also change colour to blend in.

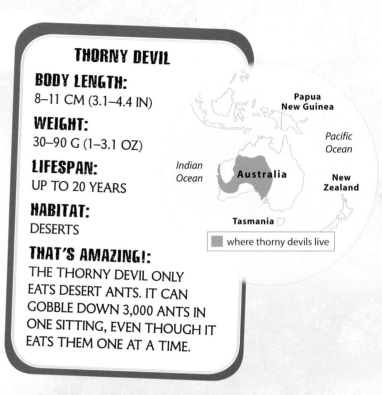

THORNY DEVIL

BODY LENGTH:
8–11 CM (3.1–4.4 IN)

WEIGHT:
30–90 G (1–3.1 OZ)

LIFESPAN:
UP TO 20 YEARS

HABITAT:
DESERTS

THAT'S AMAZING!:
THE THORNY DEVIL ONLY EATS DESERT ANTS. IT CAN GOBBLE DOWN 3,000 ANTS IN ONE SITTING, EVEN THOUGH IT EATS THEM ONE AT A TIME.

Papua New Guinea
Pacific Ocean
Indian Ocean
Australia
New Zealand
Tasmania

where thorny devils live

false head

The thorny devil has a spiny false head on the back of its neck. Predators are often tricked into eating its false head.

Water supply

In the dry **desert,** the thorny devil has a clever way of getting water. It gets liquid from dew that collects on its skin at night. The dew runs along thousands of tiny grooves in the thorny devil's skin and collects in its mouth so that it can drink it.

Thorny devils can puff themselves up to make them seem larger and more scary.

Animals in danger

Many animals in Australasia are in danger of dying out forever. When an animal dies out, it is said to be **extinct**. Animals are dying out because people are destroying their **habitats**, capturing them for pets, or killing them for their skins, meat, and body parts.

The numbat is a rabbit-sized **marsupial**. Its coat is reddish-brown with white stripes on its back. It feeds on termites. Today, numbats are under threat because their forest habitat is being cleared to make space for building. Some forests have been destroyed by wildfires. The numbat is also hunted by foxes and wild cats which were brought to Australia from Europe over 200 years ago.

The numbat lives in forests and woodlands in south-west Australia.

The number of loggerhead turtles in Australia is dropping.

Loggerhead turtles live on **coral reefs** around the northern coast of Australia. Some turtles **mate** and nest on the southern part of the Great Barrier Reef. But as the reef is put in danger by **pollution** and other threats, so are the turtles. The turtles are also getting caught in fishing nets and drowning.

Today, **conservation** groups are working hard to save these amazing animals.

Animal facts and figures

There are millions of different kinds of animals living all over the world. The place where an animal lives is called its **habitat**. Animals have special features, such as wings, claws, and fins. These features allow animals to survive in their habitats. Which animal do you think is the most amazing?

WOMBAT

BODY LENGTH:
90–115 CM (35.1–45.2 IN)

WEIGHT:
22–39 KG (48.4–85.8 LBS)

LIFESPAN:
10–12 YEARS

HABITAT:
WOODLANDS AND HEATHS

THAT'S AMAZING!:
A WOMBAT'S BACK IS COVERED IN VERY THICK, TOUGH SKIN WHICH IS DIFFICULT FOR OTHER ANIMALS TO BITE.

FUNNEL-WEB SPIDER

BODY LENGTH:
1.5–4.5 CM (.05–1.7 IN)

WEIGHT:
ABOUT 0.8–2 G (0.02–0.07 OZ)

LIFESPAN:
2–4 YEARS (FEMALE); 9 MONTHS (MALE)

HABITAT:
COASTAL FORESTS

THAT'S AMAZING!:
FUNNEL-WEB SPIDERS RUSH OUT OF THEIR **BURROWS** WHEN **PREY**, SUCH AS INSECTS AND LIZARDS, DISTURB THE 'TRIP LINES' AROUND THEIR WEB.

BROWN KIWI

BODY LENGTH:
UP TO 55 CM (21.6 IN)

WEIGHT:
UP TO 3.8 KG (8.4 LBS)

LIFESPAN:
40 YEARS

HABITAT:
COASTAL FORESTS; **GRASSLANDS**

THAT'S AMAZING!:
DURING THE NIGHT, A KIWI MAY ROAM ACROSS AN AREA THE SIZE OF 60 FOOTBALL PITCHES IN SEARCH OF FOOD.

BIRD OF PARADISE

BODY LENGTH:
17–120 CM (6.7–47.2 IN)

WEIGHT:
50–400 G (1.7–14 OZ)

LIFESPAN:
UP TO 30 YEARS (IN **CAPTIVITY**)

HABITAT:
RAINFOREST

THAT'S AMAZING!:
UNLIKE THE MALES, FEMALE BIRDS OF PARADISE ARE A DULL BROWN COLOUR. THIS IS USEFUL BECAUSE IT **CAMOUFLAGES** THEM WHEN THEY ARE SITTING ON THEIR NESTS.

PLATYPUS

BODY LENGTH:
UP TO 60 CM (23.6 IN)

WEIGHT:
2–5 KG (4.4–11 LBS)

LIFESPAN:
12 YEARS

HABITAT:
RIVERS AND STREAMS

THAT'S AMAZING!:
MALE PLATYPUSES HAVE POISONOUS SPURS ON THEIR BACK LEGS WHICH THEY USE IN SELF DEFENCE.

BOX JELLYFISH

BODY LENGTH:
20 CM (7.8 IN)

WEIGHT:
UP TO 2 KG (4.4 LBS)

LIFESPAN:
LESS THAN 1 YEAR

HABITAT:
COASTS

THAT'S AMAZING!:
FOR SOME REASON, SEA TURTLES ARE NOT HARMED BY BOX JELLYFISH STINGS. THEY OFTEN EAT THE JELLYFISH.

LEAFY SEA DRAGON

BODY LENGTH:
45 CM (17.5 IN)

WEIGHT:
UP TO 113 G (3.9 OZ)

LIFESPAN:
2–3 YEARS (IN **CAPTIVITY**)

HABITAT:
COASTS AND **CORAL REEFS**

THAT'S AMAZING!:
THE FEMALE SEA DRAGON LAYS HER EGGS ON THE MALE'S TAIL. HE CARRIES THEM UNTIL THEY HATCH.

TUATARA

BODY LENGTH:
40–60 CM (15.6–23.6 IN)

WEIGHT:
UP TO 1.3 KG (2.8 LBS)

LIFESPAN:
UP TO 100 YEARS

HABITAT:
ISLANDS

THAT'S AMAZING!:
MALE TUATARAS SOMETIMES LOSE THEIR TAILS IN FIGHTS, BUT AMAZINGLY THEY CAN GROW NEW ONES.

WATER-HOLDING FROG

BODY LENGTH:
40–70 MM (1.5–2.7 IN)

WEIGHT:
UP TO 20 G (0.7 OZ)

LIFESPAN:
UP TO 20 YEARS

HABITAT:
DESERTS

THAT'S AMAZING!:
THE FROG LAYS ITS EGGS IN PUDDLES LEFT AFTER IT HAS RAINED. THE TADPOLES MUST GROW AND CHANGE INTO FROGS QUICKLY BEFORE THE WATER DRIES UP AGAIN.

THORNY DEVIL

BODY LENGTH:
8–11 CM (3.1–4.4 IN)

WEIGHT:
30–90 G (1–3.1 OZ)

LIFESPAN:
UP TO 20 YEARS

HABITAT:
DESERTS

THAT'S AMAZING!:
THE THORNY DEVIL ONLY EATS DESERT ANTS. IT CAN GOBBLE DOWN 3,000 ANTS IN ONE SITTING, EVEN THOUGH IT EATS THEM ONE AT A TIME.

Find out more

Books to read

Exploring Continents: Australia, Jane Bingham (Heinemann Library, 2007)

Living Things: Adaptation, Holly Wallace (Heinemann Library, 2001)

Living Things: Survival and Change, Holly Wallace (Heinemann Library, 2001)

Websites

http://www.bbc.co.uk/nature/reallywild
Type in the name of the animal you want to learn about and find a page with lots of facts, figures, and pictures.

http://animals.nationalgeographic.com/animals
This site has information on the different groups of animals, stories of survival in different habitats, and stunning photo galleries to search through.

http://animaldiversity.ummz.umich.edu
A website run by the University of Michigan which has a huge encyclopedia of animals to search through.

http://www.mnh.si.edu
The website of the Smithsonian National Museum of Natural History, which has one of the largest natural history collections in the world.

Zoo sites
Many zoos around the world have their own websites which tell you about the animals they keep, where they come from, and how they are looked after.

Glossary

adapted when an animal has special features that help it to survive in its habitat

burrow hole in the ground or in a tree where an animal shelters

camouflage when an animal has special colours or markings which help to hide it in its habitat

captivity an animal kept in a zoo or wildlife park lives in captivity. Animals in captivity often live longer than wild animals because other animals are not trying to kill them, nor is there competition for food.

conservation saving and protecting wild animals and their habitats

continent one of seven huge pieces of land on Earth. Each continent is divided into smaller regions called countries.

coral reef huge underwater structure built by tiny sea creatures called coral polyps

desert dry, sandy region

extinct when a kind of animal dies out forever

grassland huge, open space covered in grass and bushes

habitat place where an animal lives and feeds

larvae the grub-like young of insects

mammal animal that has fur or hair and feeds its babies on milk

marsupial mammal that has a pouch where its babies feed and grow

mate when an animal makes babies with another animal

pollution waste, litter, and spilt oil that makes a place dirty and unfit to live in

predator animal that hunts and kills other animals for food

prey animal that is hunted and killed by other animals for food

rainforest thick forest growing around the equator where the weather is hot and wet

reptile animal with scaly skin that lays eggs on land

swamp area where large parts of the land are usually or always under water

tentacle long part of some sea animals' bodies which is used for feeding and gripping

Index

Australasia 4–5

baby animals 7, 15, 22
bills 11, 14, 15
birds 10–11, 12–13
birds of paradise 12–13
breathing 15
burrows 6, 7, 8, 9, 21, 31

camouflage 12, 19, 31
catching food (prey) 17
colour of animals 13, 16, 19, 20, 24
coral reef, Great Barrier 4, 27, 31

dry weather 23, 25

eating 24
eggs 10, 14, 15, 18, 21, 22
extinct animals 26–7, 31

feathers 13
fins 18
fish 18–19
food 6, 11, 18, 21, 24
frogs, water-holding 22

habitats 5, 7, 12, 28–9, 31

jellyfish, box 16–17

keeping cool 6, 8, 23
kiwi 10–11

lifespans 28–9

mammals 14–15, 31
marsupials 7, 26, 31

nostrils 11, 15
numbats 26

platypus 14–15
poison 9, 15, 17
pouches 7
prey 8, 17, 31
puffing up 25

reptiles 20–1, 31

sea dragons, leafy 18–19
size of animals 25, 28–9
skin 6
smelling food 11
spiders, funnel-web 8–9
spines 19, 20, 24
stings 16, 17
swimming 14, 18

tadpoles 22
tails 12, 20
tentacles 16, 17, 31
thorny devils 24–5
tuataras 20–1
turtles, loggerhead 27

water supply 23, 25
wombats 6–7